unrestrained;

table of contents

twenty-six marks short
pretentious
Sonder
logophile
progression
Drowning in a Sea of Sensations
Eccedentesiast
pandora box
echoes of tomorrow
at the end of the day, we're all just people

Wonderwall
transcendent love
playgirl
sadistic pleasures
star
bizzare
you may not remember, but I do
ride or die
betrayal
Galentine's Day

~acknowledgments:

Writing unrestrained has been an extraordinary journey, and it wouldn't have been possible without the support and encouragement of many incredible individuals.

First and foremost, I extend my heartfelt gratitude to my family for their unwavering belief in me and their constant encouragement. To my parents, thank you for your endless support and for always being my rock. Your faith in my abilities has been a driving force behind this book. To my sister, your quirky comments and "constructive" criticism about my writing has kept me grounded (and entertained) throughout this journey.

A special thanks to all my friends who provided me with the best support system I could ever ask for. I am deeply grateful for the late-night conversations and the motivation to push through challenging moments.

To my mentors and teachers, thank you for nurturing my love for writing and helping me refine my craft. Your guidance has been instrumental in shaping my voice and vision.

Lastly, to my dear readers, your encouragement and belief in unrestrained mean the world to me.

Thank you all for being a part of this journey.

From the desk of,

Nysa Jain.

~chapter 1: sapphire skies

twenty six marks short (but would even that be enough?)

twenty six marks short
(but would even that be enough?)

expectations weigh heavy
a silent burden of invisible chains
a pressure that seeps into every moment
every breath
every thought.
people look at me
eyes filled with hope
with dreams they crafted in my image
a reflection of their own desires
their unspoken wishes.

i walk a tightrope
balancing on the fine line
between who i am and who you want me to be.
every step measured
every move calculated
yet the ground beneath me shifts.
i may not always reach them.

those lofty heights you envision
your idealised version of me
a mirage in the distance
and when i stumble
when i fall short
the disappointment is palpable
an echo that reverberates
in the silence of your unmet expectations.

but i am more than your dreams
more than the sum of your hopes.
i am a complex mosaic

of failures and triumphs
of moments of clarity and confusion
of growth that often comes uncelebrated.

in the end,
the true achievement is not in meeting your expectations,
but in staying true to my own path,
in finding peace within the chaos,
and embracing the imperfect journey,
that is uniquely, unapologetically
mine.

pretentious

a mask worn like a crown,
invisible threads woven tight,
a gaze that pierces through
the ordinary,
claiming truth where none is sought.

words spill out,
a river of polished stones,
smooth to the touch,
but hollow within.
they tumble over each other,
chasing meaning that evades
even the one who speaks.

a hand raised,
not in question, but in proclamation,
to be seen, to be heard,
to fill the air with something
other than silence.

eyes scan the room,
seeking the reflection of their own
brilliance,
a need to be affirmed,
to be known,
to be more than just a name.

but beneath the surface,
a quiet tremor,
a whisper that goes unheard—
the fear of being seen,
not as a beacon,
but as a flicker,
a momentary light
in a vast, indifferent night.

Sonder

In fleeting glances, lives unfold,
Worlds untold, stories bold.
Silent whispers of dreams and fears,
In every heart, laughter, and tears.

A glance exchanged, a soul revealed,
Moments lived, emotions concealed.
Each passerby, a universe deep,
Words bittersweet, memories to keep.

The crowd's hum, a symphony,
Of lives entwined, endlessly.
In the tapestry of humanity,
Sonder blooms in shared infinity.

logophile

in the quiet corners of my mind,
where whispers weave and words unwind,
a realm of letters, soft and grand,
where every phrase, a strand in hand.

i gather nouns like seashells bright,
each one a gem, a glint of light,
verbs like rivers, swift and free,
flow through the pages endlessly.

adjectives, with colours bold,
paint the stories yet untold,
while adverbs dance in rhythmic song,
guiding the way, where thoughts belong.

in syllables, I find my peace,
a world where all distractions cease,
each sentence, like a bridge to dreams,
built with passion, hope, and schemes.

i swim in paragraphs so deep,
where ancient tales and secrets sleep,
in every book, a universe,
a symphony in every verse.

for in these words, I come alive,
they shape the way I think, I strive,
a logophile, in love with sound,
in every letter, joy is found.

so let me dwell where stories grow,
where every thought, a seed to sow,
in this garden of the mind,
i seek, i find, i am defined.

progression

we've progressed from periods to blocs to lectures
we've gone from sharing tiffin boxes and having playdates to eating
on our own and fighting over boys that are indifferent
we've gone from being kept awake by our dreams of the future and
what's to come to having nightmares about failure and dreading
waking up the next day
we've gone from handmade friendship bracelets made of loom bands to
expecting expensive jewellery from boys that won't give them to us,
that don't care enough to go that extra mile
we've gone from running to our parents for every little thing to trying
to learn to be independent, stumbling a little along the way but
persevering nonetheless
we're younger, but we're old
we're older, but we're young
we're everything and nothing and never and all at once
we love to hurt and hurt to love
we're the same, but different
we're different, but the same
progression, a better word for change

Drowning in a Sea of Sensations

The world hums with a constant buzz,
A mix of sounds and lights,
A stream of experiences flowing by.
It's a lot to take in, a wave that sometimes
Threatens to pull me under.

Love, powerful and ever-present,
Can lift me up and ground me in equal measure.
It's a steady force, beautiful yet complex,
A reminder of how delicate our connections can be.

I seek moments of calm,
A pause in the rhythm,
A space to breathe and find my centre again.
But the world moves forward,
Its pulse unchanging,
And I'm learning to move with it,
Finding my pace amidst the currents.

I think of simpler times,
When life felt less crowded,
But those are memories now,
A glimpse into what was.
So I focus on navigating the now,
Balancing in the midst of it all,
Seeing the beauty around me
And recognising the weight it carries.

Eccedentesiast

The eccedentesiast knows,
The art of pretending,
The craft of camouflage,
Of blending into the tapestry of expected joy.

But in the quiet corners,
Away from the crowd,
The facade crumbles,
And the weight is finally felt.

Yet, the world turns a blind eye,
Preferring the comfort of illusions,
For the truth is too raw,
Too real, too uncomfortable to bear.

So the show goes on,
A continuous act of endurance,
A dance of silent suffering,
Masked by a smile that never quite reaches the eyes.

pandora box

you're a walking talking pandora box
you eat up my lies like ants devour sugar syrup on a summer day
i feel sorry for you
you fell for me, but you don't even know who i am
we only just met, and i barely know myself
i label you, and judge you for every small stumble you make while
tracing the arc of us
you label us, say we're in a relationship, say you're in love
you perplex me, and i'm not sure why
i'm not sure who the true pandora box is
you or i.

echoes of tomorrow

the smell of earth after it rains.
charcoal drawings.
braids.
long conversations late at night.
quiet afternoons spent listening to music.
baking with family and licking the chocolate from the spoon.
love letters.
open windows.
getting so absorbed in a book that you forget the world exists.
taking too many pictures.
warm sunlight on your skin on a chilly day.
the smell of old books.
screaming at the top of your lungs on rollercoasters.
handmade gifts.
feeling the dirt underneath your fingernails when you climb
mountains.
the smell of old books.
laughing till your stomach aches and your jaw hurts.
having unapologetic fun.
falling in love.
knowing that tomorrow is a new day, and *you* are in control.

at the end of the day, we're all just people

we're not as different as i thought, the boys and us
they'd put everything on the line for love,
as we would for trust

it's always at the back of my mind
that niggling feeling of doubt
i don't know what i'm expecting to find

at the end of the day, we're all just people
we all want to feel wanted,
we all want that glory and fame
we're humans, one and the same.

Wonderwall

I saw you standing there,
a moment stretched in sunlight,
the world around us blurred,
colours melting, sounds fading.
You were clear, sharp,
a beacon in the haze.

Your eyes, an ocean,
infinite and deep,
pulled me in,
and I was lost
without wanting to be found.

Time played tricks,
slowing, stuttering,
as if the universe itself
held its breath
in reverence
of this,
this instant
when everything
changed.

Your smile,
a quiet revelation,
unfurled like a secret
whispered to the heart,
so soft,
yet so loud
it drowned out
every doubt,
every fear,
every shadow.

I didn't know your name,
your story,
or the paths
that led you here,
but it didn't matter.
In that fleeting gaze,
I saw the possibility
of forever,
etched in the spaces
between us.

The air grew thick
with unspoken words,
a symphony of what-ifs
and maybe-somedays.
I breathed you in,
let the wonder
settle in my bones,
and knew
I would never be the same.

You, a wonderwall,
standing tall,
unchanged,
as the world spun on.
And I,
forever altered,
by the simple,
unexpected
grace
of seeing you
for the first time.

transcendent love

did he tell you
even when you weren't together that he would always be there?

did he make sure
you knew that he loved you, you felt it, everytime he said it?

did he try and try and try
to work at something that was doomed from the beginning?

if yes,
i am beyond happy for you,
and i wish you both all the very best in life.

and if not,
know that our love was transcendent,
and he's not done healing.
don't let him go just yet,
he might not try as hard this time.

playgirl

feeling salty isn't gonna get you anywhere
i've made my share of empty promises
but we both had a part to play
it takes two to tango
two to clap
two to make a pair

and two to get us *there*
i know it isn't fair
time has stolen the details a bit
but it's for the best
you know it is.

sadistic pleasures

what sadistic pleasure do you get? telling him that he should be wary?
is it a twisted dance of jealousy,
or a last resort to preserve our love?
do you relish in the chaos that you cause,
as you whisper caution to his eager ears?
perhaps i got it wrong
perhaps it's simply a lingering echo
of your own fears and insecurities,
manifested in this futile attempt
to derail my future niceties

you're driving on a dead-end street
he's a fool in love
little do i know
your words in his ears
will ring more than i thought

star

you think you're such a star but you're really not
if only you could yourself from my eyes
maybe your ego will deflate a little
or maybe a lot

always on about how you hate someone
who hasn't even said a word to you
always putting me down and making me feel like a fool

you think you're such a star but you're really not

bizarre

we were living in a fantasy
a miridical unreality
kissing in trampoline parks
always together, never apart

with his promiscuous actions
and my chain reactions
our love had no bounds
it's crazy to think we're over now

you may not remember, but i do

i vividly remember the day you told me you fell in love with me
it was 7th grade, halfway through july
in the middle of the indian monsoon
the grey clouds gathered
a distant rumble
a thunderous sound
my friends and i raced out of the school gate, holding hands and giggling
flaunting that there was no chance we were letting one drop of the cascading shower touch our bodies but knowing we wanted to anyway
first, a drizzle, gentle and light,
i see you come out the gate with all your boys
you see me and smile
i let out a hearty laugh as the shower turns into a torrent
falling with a mighty roar
we dance in the street
our bare feet splashing to a rhythmic beat
the air is filled with a fragrant scent
of wet earth and flowers
you step towards me and splash rain on my face
i smirk and aim a kick of murky puddle-water towards yours
i miss terribly and end up kicking you instead
but you don't mind
you smile and wave goodbye as we jostle into our separate buses and ride home
in hindsight it seems stupid, immature even
you fell in love with me when i kicked you?
how absurd.
but you and i both know it was more than that
only we saw the sneaky glances, flushed faces and dewy eyes
only we knew how much it meant, how much love our hearts surmised
the storm fades to a gentle mist
the sun breaks through, its rays kissed by rainbows arching in the sky
i'll never forget this day, even though our love has died

ride or die

when i'm planning a party
you're the first person i put on the invite list

when the walls are closing in
you're the only person who doesn't make me feel like shit

when he bitches and spreads stuff
you're the only one that doesn't believe it

when i'm at the lowest point in my life
you're the one who's on my side

you're the one that i call when it's 2 in the morning
and i'm in bed crying

but where are you now
probably at squash
i know you work hard
but at our friendship you're not

i'm not sure what happened
between us at all
all i know is i miss you
but you won't even call

you're one of my oldest friends
we first met when we were only 12 years old
and i don't know how to fix this because
we've never even fought before.

betrayal

for you i'd take a bullet
myself i would surrender
but roles reversed
you'd be friends with my murderer

in the dance of shadows
where loyalty lies,
i'd take a bullet
without goodbyes.

call me dramatic,
call me insane,
but at least i'd stick up for you
why can't you do the same?

i'd cut off anyone that hurt you
wouldn't think twice
i shouldn't have to beg for you to do the same
but even that won't suffice

i know that i don't own u
and i never will,
i can't control you
but sure, keep things chill
he hurt me, not you
my scars will never fully heal
and my anger when ur with him,
i have no right to feel

i just need some space
the betrayal hasn't sinked in
even after destroying everything,
he's still the one that wins

heartache won't dissipate
so display it, i wont
i know i have no right to feel it
but it doesn't mean i don't

Galentine's Day

I may not buy you gifts today
Or think to send you flowers
But I know just what you like very well
And we've laughed and talked for hours

I don't see you as much as I used to
But I often think of you
And though we don't share a roof
You're still my family too

Time has stolen the details a bit
But I'm always an open book
Even when there are no words
You 'get it' with just a look

You're not the one who holds my hand
Or the one I greet at the door
But you've held my broken heart
And you know me to my core

We've sat in amphitheaters
Sometimes joyful, sometimes in pain
Its not a romance novel
But a love note all the same

Our friendship just gets stronger
Even distance holds as close
And when I have news, important or not
You come to mind the most

A cannot-be-without-you love
To the earth, and its ends
So every year this day rolls around
I think about my friends

Galentine's Day, with memories bright,
Through highs and lows, our journey we trace,
I am eternally grateful for people like you
Forever bound, in friendship's embrace.

it all started with a hi

you gaze to the street, your hands in your pockets
my outspoken, extroverted self holds out an outstretched hand
"hi."
i introduce myself and ask if you're here for maths.
you tell me your name, say yes.
i smile.
"waiting for a friend," you say.
i nod and tell you i'll see you inside.

in that moment, we knew nothing at all
just strangers passing by, answering fate's call
two lives intersecting, unaware of the thread
that would weave us together, where paths once led

we became friends,
in the simplest of ways
shared secrets and laughter through countless days
slowly, the quiet of love took root
in the spaces between us, tender and acute

but time, as it does, wore thin our bond
the love that once flourished, now nearly gone
from strangers to lovers, and back once more
two hearts that had danced, now unsure of the score

now, here we stand, where it all began
your gaze on the street, my outstretched hand
but this time, the words don't come as they should

we're strangers again, as if we never could
recall the warmth, the closeness we knew
in this moment, what's left feels distant, askew

but deep down, a part of me clings to that start
when we knew nothing but followed our heart

pistanthrophobia

the fear of trusting people due to past experiences with relationships
gone bad
trust wanes, heart recoils, distance.
loneliness looms,
jealousy seeps,
solitude.

muscle memory

you said that for you i always come first place
but for me, you're the only one in the race

i have you memorised.
your soft smile, one dimple,
the way you style your hair,
your laugh that makes your whole body shake,
the crinkles next to your eyes,
your hands that fit so perfectly with mine,
your warm chest,
your strong shoulders,
your gentle touch.
i know your voice,
i've learned your scent,
it lingers long after you've left.

i've got you locked in muscle memory,
the way your embrace feels like home,
the rhythm of your heartbeat against mine,
like a song I never want to forget.
so even when you're not here,
i can close my eyes,
and there you are,in every fiber of my being,
as if you never left.

birthday

your birthday's in december.
today is the eleventh of march.
and ive already planned your birthday gift.
here's a note, to start

"i love your obsession with bollywood
and how we can listen to music for hours,
i love spending time with you,
on your terrace, looking at the stars
i love the effort you make
to make sure no one feels left out
i love it when you say my name
and call me yours, without a doubt
i love how much you try,
and okay, call me deranged
but you're perfect just the way you are
and i hope you never change"

17 gifts for your 17th birthday
that's what i had planned
how we got here, the kind of mess we're in
ill never understand.

bus rides

i sling one arm across your shoulder
you fall asleep on my chest
i play with your hair
and stare at you while you rest
we sing our hearts out
and play card games all night
we sit close
not just two hands
but two hearts intertwined
our friendship was simple
but our love is abstract
i love you like this but i like you like that

unfair

its not fair.

we've tried it your way for months now
we've sat in silence, our feelings buried inside
and not spoken a word, for fear of crossing a line.

we've been friends, but we've touched.
we've held hands, and we've pretended not to care as much.

why can't we just try for once?

i'm not saying we have to be each other's forever loves,
all i'm saying is we can try.

every single time we've fought so far
has been about who's way,
yours or mine.

Love Language

Love doesn't always speak
in clear, loud voices.
Sometimes it's in the quiet,
in the spaces between words.
A touch that lingers,
a gaze that holds,
unspoken understandings
that fill the gaps.

It's not always grand
or dramatic.
It's in the small moments,
in patience practiced,
in forgiveness given freely.
Love breathes in the mundane,
in the everyday rituals
that build a life together.

It's in the way you listen,
the way you stand close,
the way you understand
without needing to be told.
It's in the smiles shared
across rooms,
the gentle reminders
of presence and care.

In the stillness of a shared space,
in the quiet comfort of being near,
love speaks softly,
whispering in actions,
in the delicate dance of routine.
It's the language
that needs no translation,
the one that's always understood
even when it's not said out loud.

pointless

this futile
attempt to reconcile
left me with nothing
but a fake smile

we try to find a bridge
to span the growing gap
but every step we take
only leads us further back

we speak of dreams and plans
of things we hoped to be
but those dreams have faded
lost to the shifting sea

our laughter has gone quiet
replaced by awkward sighs
tears fall softly down
as love, unseen, slowly dies

we chase a setting sun
hoping to bring back light
but night falls all around
and we're swallowed by the night

in this futile attempt
to fix what once was whole
we part with heavy hearts
two halves of a broken soul

claw clip

i changed the way my table faces
to get a new perspective but
it's not liked it worked
it's not like it changed anything
now i'm holding my hair back and searching all around my room for
my claw clip before i realise that you took it
on the school trip
when i rested my head on your shoulder
i let my hair loose
because that's how i fall asleep
and i didn't have a bag so i put my claw clip in yours
and you never gave it back
i miss it
i wish i had it right now
but not so much because i need it
more because
it hurts to have a part of me with you
even if it's a very small part.

every moment away from you feels wrong
memories of our time together play on a loop in my mind, like a never
ending record player, reminding me of the love we had for one
another.

now, those same fond memories are bittersweet
i long to talk to you for hours on end, to hear your laughter at
something I said, to see the sparkle in your eyes once more.

until then, I replace my claw clip with a rubber band, and hope one
day you'll find it in your room and reminisce about what we had.

If death had a flavour

If death had a flavour, it would be less sour
Than the day we last talked, in that fateful hour.
Your words cut deep, sharper than a knife,
Leaving scars that linger, haunting my life.

The silence that followed was colder than death,
A void filled with memories, taking my breath.
Each recollection, a dagger to my heart,
Reminding me painfully that we're worlds apart.

If death had a scent, it would be less cruel
Than the smell of our love burning down to fuel.
For regret's fire consumes every night,
Leaving ashes of dreams once so bright.

Your name on my lips now tastes bitter and cold,
A taste that lingers, a story retold.
Each syllable drips with sorrow and pain,
A reminder of joy that will never remain.

If death had a touch, it would be less cold
Than the chill in my bones from the lies you once told.
Your absence is a shadow, dark and vast,
A haunting reminder of a love that couldn't last.

In the garden of memory, where sorrow has grown,
I wander alone, with seeds of regret sown.
For even if death claimed me, I'd still say
It's less sour than the hurt of our last shared day

~playlist

1. Paris by The Chainsmokers

2. making the bed by Olivia Rodrigo

3. 16 by Baby Keem

4. All Too Well (10 Minute Version) [Taylor's Version] [From The Vault] by Taylor Swift

5. Sunflower (Spider-Man: Into the Spider-Verse) by Post Malone & Swae Lee

6. BIRDS OF A FEATHER by Billie Eilish

7. A Sky Full of Stars by Coldplay

8. Block me out by Gracie Abrams

9. Riptide by Vance Joy

10. reckless driving by Lizzy McAlpine (feat. Ben Kessler)